# History of A
The Settling of America

1590 to 1754

Sally Senzell Isaacs

Heinemann
LIBRARY

First published in Great Britain by Heinemann Library,
Halley Court, Jordan Hill, Oxford OX2 8EJ
a division of Reed Educational and Professional Publishing Ltd.
Heinemann is a registered trademark of Reed Educational & Professional Publishing Limited. Oxford, Melbourne, Auckland, Johannesburg, Blantyre, Gaborone, Ibadan, Portsmouth (NH) USA, Chicago

© Bender Richardson White 1998
© Illustrations: Bender Richardson White 1998
The moral right of the proprietor has been asserted.

All rights reserved. No part of this publication may be reproduced or transmitted in any form or by any means, electronic or mechanical, including photocopying, recording, taping, or any information retrieval system, without permission in writing from the publisher or a licence permitting restricted copying in the United Kingdom issued by the Copyright Licensing Agency Ltd, 90 Tottenham Court Road, London WIP OLP.

THE SETTLING OF AMERICA
was produced for Heinemann Library
by Bender Richardson White.

Editor: Lionel Bender
Designer: Ben White
Assistant Editor: Michael March
Picture Researcher: Madeleine Samuel
Media Conversion and Typesetting: MW Graphics
Production Controller: Kim Richardson

03 02 01 00 99
10 9 8 7 6 5 4 3 2 1

Printed in Hong Kong

British Library Cataloguing-in-Publication Data.
Isaacs, Sally Senzell
   History of America : 1595 – 1750 Settling of America
   1. United States - History - Colonial period, ca. 1600 – 1775
   – Juvenile literature
   I. Title.
   973.2

ISBN 0431 05641 2 Hb   ISBN 0431 05646 3 Pb

Special thanks to Mike Carpenter, Scott Westerfield and Tristan Boyer at Heinemann Library for editorial and design guidance and direction.

Any words appearing in the text in bold, **like this**, are explained in the Glossary.

Photo Credits:
Bridgeman Art Library: page 7 top (British Museum, London), 38 (National Maritime Museum, London. Picture Research Consultants Consultants, Mass.: pages 7 bottom (Library of Congress), 8 top and 8 bottom (Library of Congress), 12 top (Colonial Williamsburg Foundation), 12 bottom (Farrell Grehan, © National Geographic Society), 16 (Library of Congress), 17 (Virginia State Library), 18 top, 18 bottom (Private Collection), 20 top (Plimouth Plantation), 20 bottom (Library of Congress), 27 (Public Archives of Canada), 30 top (The Bancroft Library, University of California, Berkeley), 32 (Museum of the American Numismatic Association), 33 (New York Public Library/Astor, Lenox, and Tilden Foundations), 35 top (Ohio Historical Society). Peter Newark's American/Military Pictures: pages 10, 15 bottom, 23 left, 23 right, 25, 29 bottom, 35 bottom, 36 top, 36 bottom, 39, 40, 41. North Wind Picture Archives: pages 11, 15 top, 31 bottom
Werner Forman Archive: page 29 top (Museum fur Volkerkunde, Berlin).

Every effort has been made to contact copyright holders of any material reproduced in this book. Omissions will be rectified in subsequent printings if notice is given to the publisher.

Artwork credits
Illustrations by: John James on pages 6/7, 8/9, 14/15, 20/21, 26/27, 30/31, 32/33, 36/37, 38/39; James Field on pages 24/25, 40/41; Mark Bergin on pages 10/11, 16/17, 28/29; Gerald Wood on pages 18/19. 34/35: Nick Hewetson on pages 12/13, 22/23. Maps by Stefan Chabluk.
Cover: Design and make-up by Pelican Graphics. Artwork by John James. Photos: Top and Centre: North Wind Picture Archives. Bottom: Peter Newark's American Pictures.

Major quotations used in this book come from the following sources. Some of the quotations have been abridged for clarity:
Page 6: Words from a 1600s play from *A History of US* by Joy Hakim. New York: Oxford University Press, 1993, Book 2, Page 18.
Page 10: Powhatan 1609 speech reported by John Smith. Taken from *I Have Spoken - American History through the Voices of Indians* compiled by Virginia Irving Armstrong. Sage Books, 1971, page 10.
Page 18: William Bradford quote from *Colonial Histories, Massachusetts* by James Playsted Woods. Nashville: Thomas Nelson, Inc., 1969, page 20.
Page 22: John Winthrop quote from *The History of New England* (John Winthrop's *Journal*). Taken from *Colonial Histories - Massachusetts* by James Playsted Wood. Nashville: Thomas Nelson, Inc., 1969, page 48.
Page 30: Iroquois Red Jacket. quote from *Native American Testimony*, page 69, . Edited by Peter Nabokov. New York: Thomas Y. Crowell, 1978. Credited to: *Indian Biography* by B.B. Thatcher. New York. 1845.
Page 38: Slavery quote from *The Interesting Narrative of the Life of Olaudah Equiano* written by himself. First published in1789 – from an abridgement: *Equiano's Travels* edited by Paul Edwards. New York, Washington: Frederick A. Praeger Publishers, 1967, page 31.

The Consultants
Special thanks to Diane Smolinski, Nancy Cope and Christopher Gibb for their help in the preparation of this book.

Contents

ABOUT THIS BOOK		4
THE UNITED STATES OF AMERICA—MAP		4
INTRODUCTION		5

A VILLAGE BY THE RIVER — 6
1590 to 1607
The sign of the Five Iroquois Nations founded in 1570

THE ENGLISH ARRIVE — 8
1607 to 1608
The seal of Virginia Colony

PROTECTING THEIR LAND — 10
1607 to 1609
Metal helmets worn by colonists in battles

LIFE IN JAMESTOWN — 12
1608 to 1613
An illustration from a Virginia Colony broadsheet

POCAHONTAS MARRIES — 14
1613 to 1617
A 17th-century English transatlantic sailing ship

VIRGINIA PLANTATIONS — 16
1619 to 1622
A tobacco plant in leaf and flower

THE MAYFLOWER ARRIVES — 18
1620 to 1622
Barrels from Plymouth Colony, Massachusetts

A HOME IN THE COLONIES — 20
1640 to 1680
A colonist's wood-axes for cutting and shaping timber

GROWING TOWNS — 22
1630 to 1680
A Boston "pine tree" shilling coin

NEW NETHERLANDS — 24
1609 to 1664
The New Amsterdam coat-of-arms

NEW FRANCE — 26
1603 to 1683
The French flag of 1603, with the fleur-de-lys emblem

WEST OF THE COLONIES — 28
1680s to 1700s
Eagle feathers worn as headdress by Native Americans

MISSIONS IN THE WEST — 30
1598 to late 1700s
A wooden cross from a Catholic mission

THE SHOPS OF BOSTON — 32
1700 to 1750
A Massachusetts' silver teapot of 1740

GETTING THINGS DONE — 34
1700 to 1735
A Benjamin Franklin book, spectacles, and pamphlet

FARMING AND FOOD — 36
1730 to 1750
A 1750s image respecting the plow as a farmer's tool

SLAVERY — 38
1730 to 1750
Iron slave-chains from Africa

CITY LIFE — 40
1730 to 1754
A wealthy family's house in Alexandria, Virginia, in 1755

HISTORICAL MAP OF AMERICA	42
FAMOUS PEOPLE OF THE TIME	44
IMPORTANT DATES AND EVENTS	44
GLOSSARY	46
MORE BOOKS TO READ	47
PLACES TO VISIT	47
INDEX	47

ABOUT THIS SERIES

History of America is a series of nine books arranged chronologically, meaning that events are described in the order in which they happened. However, since each book focuses on an important person in American history, the timespans of the titles overlap. In each book, most articles deal with a particular event or part of American history. Others deal with aspects of everyday life, such as trade, houses, clothing and farming. These general articles cover longer periods of time. The little illustrations at the top left of each article are a symbol of the times. They are identified on page 3.

▼ About the map
This map shows the United States today. It shows the boundaries and names of all the states. Refer to this map, or to the one on pages 42–43, to locate places talked about in this book.

About this book

This book is about America from 1590 to 1754. The term America means 'the United States of America'. Some historians refer to the native people of America as Amerinds or Indians, as Christopher Columbus did. Others call them Native Americans, as we do.

For about ten years, a young Native American girl, Pocahontas, was the focal point of the early settlement of America. This book describes and illustrates her life history as an introduction to gradual settling of America. Historians are not sure exactly when Pocahontas was born. Based on the opinions of many historians, this book assumes she was born in 1596. Words in **bold** are explained in more detail in the glossary on page 46.

INTRODUCTION

Pocahontas was a young Native American girl whose life bridged the two worlds of European settlers and Native Americans. In 1596, when Pocahontas was born, America was mostly a land of wide-open spaces and small Native American villages. Eastern Native Americans paddled up rivers in bark canoes. Native Americans of the **Great Plains** chased after buffalo herds. Totem poles dotted the villages of the North-west Coast Native Americans. However, the Native Americans were no longer alone. First explorers, then **settlers** came from France, England the Netherlands, and Spain. These European countries were determined to have **colonies** in America. The country could send settlers to the colonies, bring back wealth from them and govern them from a distance.

This book describes how America grew from clumps of huts along the James River to thriving Virginia **plantations** and bustling towns such as Boston and Philadelphia. As time passed, American life moved further west. The book tells the story of brave Europeans who left everything to start a new life in the New World. It also shows how the lives of Native Americans were for ever changed and exploited by the early settlers, who came with guns as well as gifts.

For about ten years in the early 1600s, a young princess of the Powhatan **tribe** helped bring about cooperation between her people and the early settlers. Her name was Pocahontas. Events in the first part of this book took place during Pocahontas's lifetime. Later events happened after her death. On pages that describe events during the life of Pocahontas or her family, yellow boxes summarize what they were doing at the time.

1590 to 1607

A Village by the River

"I tell thee, gold is more plentiful there than copper is with us, and as for rubies and diamonds, they gather them by the seashore, to hang on their children's coats." This is how a London play in the 1600s described America. The words of the play were quite inaccurate.

The Powhatan **tribe** lived in villages in what is now Virginia. The tribe's chief was named Powhatan. In 1596, Powhatan's daughter, Pocahontas, was born. In her village, crops grew well in the soil. Fish swam through the rivers. Deer, rabbits and turkeys lived in the forests. The women planted fields of corn and vegetables. The men hunted, fished and fought wars with other tribes. The children learned by helping the adults.

Pocahontas

Princess Pocahontas was one of Chief Powhatan's many children. Like all her people, she had a secret name, known only within her tribe. That name was Matoax. It meant 'Little Snow Feather'.

Pocohontas spent her days like the other Native American girls. They woke early and ran down to the river to watch the sun rise. Then they danced and sang to their gods.

Because Pocahontas was a princess, she probably did not help with the planting as other girls did. Most likely her work included sewing skins together for her skirts and gathering flowers for her hair.

◀ **Colonist** and artist John White drew this picture of an Algonquin village in the late 1500s. The Algonquin and Powhatan tribes lived by East Coast rivers. They covered their **longhouses** with woven reeds or pieces of bark, which were rolled up in the summer to allow a cool breeze into the houses.

Growing corn

Corn was the most important food for the Powhatan people. Women planted it, picked it and ground the kernels into meal. They used the meal to make cornbread. After all the corn was picked, the village gathered to celebrate. Everyone danced around huge bonfires. Children held racing and leaping contests. The men sang songs about the brave things their tribe had done.

The Powhatan knew how and where to plant plentiful crops. In time, this skill would be envied by the English **settlers** who would arrive at nearby Jamestown.

◀ Native Americans in the North-east made houses, baskets and baby carriers from twigs, grasses and reeds. They made moccasins and clothes from animal skins, and sewing needles and fishing hooks from animal bones. Animal meat was a main source of food.

◀ This picture appeared on a map drawn by John Smith in 1612. It shows Chief Powhatan talking to his people in a longhouse.
Powhatan became a chief when his older brother died in 1570. His kingdom at the time included five or six tribes – about 1000 people. Powhatan wanted a larger kingdom. He took over at least 22 other tribes. By 1607, he ruled more than 8500 people. Powhatan was a respected but tough leader. He believed in harsh punishments.

1607 to 1608

THE ENGLISH ARRIVE

The five-month journey from England to Virginia was over. Three ships sailed up the James River with 105 men aboard. Most of them signed up for the journey because they were looking for an adventure. Only a few could hunt, build houses or farm.

The men had a business arrangement with the Virginia Company of London. The company gave them the opportunity to settle in a new **colony**. In return, the men were supposed to send back gold or other valuables they found in Virginia. Problems began immediately. The ships arrived at Jamestown in May 1607, three months later than expected. The passengers had eaten most of the food that should have been saved for Virginia. They arrived too late to plant crops.

▶ Before long, the **colonists** desperately needed food. They went to the Powhatan and gave them glass beads, bells, brass pans, metal hatchets, saws and axes. In return, the Powhatan gave the colonists corn and meat. Some of the Native Americans were friendly. Others did not trust the newcomers. The Powhatan wanted to own English guns. That was one thing the Englishmen would never give them!

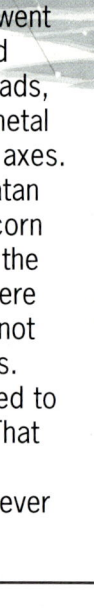

A struggle to survive

The **settlers** dug one-room mud huts into the side of a hill for somewhere to live. They built a fort with five cannons at each corner. They named their colony James Fort, after England's King James I.

John Smith became the colony's leader. He was a hard worker. He also knew how to get along with the Powhatan people. He learned their language. He took English goods to their villages and traded them for corn.

By August 1607, the food the colonists had brought from England ran out, the drinking water was polluted and mosquitoes were everywhere. Nearly half the settlers had died. By September, only 59 were alive. By January 1608, there were just 38 settlers left. But with help from the Powhatan, the colony survived.

▲ This **engraving** of John Smith was made in 1616 by colonist Simon Van der Pass.

▼ Native Americans planting seeds – in a book illustration of 1591 by Theodore De Bry.

▲ John Smith made friends with Pocahontas by showing her a compass and giving her glass beads.

Pocahontas meets John Smith

Of all the Powhatan people, 11-year-old Pocahontas seemed least afraid of the settlers. Before she ever met John Smith, she was fascinated with daring stories about him. After they met, she enjoyed learning his language and teaching him her language.

▼ Jamestown is located on the James River in Virginia.

1607 to 1609

PROTECTING THEIR LAND

"Take away your guns and swords, the cause of all our jealousy, or you may die in the same manner." Chief Powhatan gave this speech in 1609. As time went on, Powhatan grew less patient and less trusting of the English. Had they not come to trade for corn then go home? So when were they leaving?

It looked as if the English were planning to stay for a long time. They were clearing the forests and building homes, a fort and a church. Could Native Americans and English **settlers** live together peacefully? It seemed unlikely. There were big differences between Native Americans and Europeans.

One important difference was their idea about land. To the Native Americans, land could not be owned. It belonged to everyone, like the sky, air and water. The Europeans believed land could be owned, much like one owned a rifle or a hatchet. Now, they wanted to own the land and waters of Powhatan villages. The Native Americans would not allow this.

John Smith is captured

In December 1607, a group of Powhatan captured John Smith. They took him to their chief. What happened next is unclear. Smith wrote one version of the story. Chief Powhatan planned to have him killed, said Smith. Just then "Pocahontas, the King's dearest daughter, when no **entreaty** could prevail, got his head in her arms, and laid her own upon his to save him from death; whereat the Emperor was contented he should live."

▼ This man is armed with a 'matchlock' musket used by the English in 1607. The drawing is by Jacob de Ghyen. The Powhatan were fascinated by the English guns and cannons. They called them 'thunder weapons'.

Pocahontas's feelings

John Smith claimed that Pocahontas saved his life. Some historians do not believe Smith's story. They say that Powhatan did not plan to kill Smith. He had asked Pocahontas to act out this rescue scene. It was his way of showing respect for Smith.

No matter which story is true, the rescue was important to Pocahontas. In Native American tradition, when a captive is saved from death, the captive is forever 'family' to the tribe. Pocahontas was pleased that Smith would now be her 'brother'.

▲ The settlers believed this part of Virginia was England's land now. They had plenty of guns to defend it. They built a three-sided fort with a high fence around it for protection against the Native Americans.

◀ This picture appeared in John Smith's book *Generall Historie of Virginia*. The book was written in 1624. In the picture, Powhatan – seated on the right – watches as Smith is about to be killed. Pocahontas – standing in front – is begging to save his life.

▲ Settlers and Native Americans fought each other often. The settlers fought with guns, metal axes and swords. The Native Americans had clubs, bows and arrows, and spears.

▲ The Native Americans hid in the forests and attacked the fort when their opponents least expected it. The English thought this was cowardly.

11

1608 to 1613

Life in Jamestown

New Year's Day, 1608, was no celebration for the 38 surviving colonists at James Fort. Most of them were at death's door. Then, on 2 January, three ships arrived from England. They brought much-needed food and 150 new colonists.

Five days later, disaster struck. A fire raged through James Fort. It destroyed many of the huts and the church. Worst of all, the new supply of food was lost. John Smith and other **colony** leaders turned to Powhatan for help. They brought copper kettles, hatchets, knives, scissors and blue glass beads. Powhatan took these things and gave the **colonists** the corn they wanted. At another time, Powhatan traded turkeys for English swords. Trading was not easy. Often the two sides argued about fair trading. Pocahontas helped the two sides get along.

In October 1609, John Smith met more bad luck. He was carrying a bag of gunpowder when it exploded. Smith was badly burned. He sailed back to London where doctors could help him.

Once Smith left, the Indians and colonists fought bitterly. There seemed to be no hope for the colonists. The winter of 1609–1610 was called the 'Starving Time'. The colonists ran out of food. But just as James Fort's last 60 people were ready to sail off to Canada, two more ships arrived. The colony got a second chance. In 1610, the colonists changed the name of James Fort to Jamestown, as it is known today.

Pocahontas keeps the peace
Pocahontas was friends with her people and the settlers. When the two sides fought, she persuaded them to be peaceful. She often went to James Fort to bring the settlers corn and turkeys.

She loved visiting John Smith. He was amusing, clever and caring. In 1609, she heard that John Smith was no longer in James Fort. She thought he was dead. She was very sad.

▼ A settlers' metal helmet, found near Jamestown.

▶ Parts of Jamestown have been recreated next to the site of the original **settlement**. Visitors can see full-scale models of the ships that brought the colonists, as well as a Powhatan **longhouse** and the colonists' simple houses.

▶ Following the fire, the settlers tried to build a better colony. They enlarged the fort and built sturdier houses with wood frames. They dug a deep well to get more drinking water. They now copied the Powhatan, planting corn, beans and pumpkins.

13

1613 to 1617
POCAHONTAS MARRIES

In the spring of 1613, the settlers kidnapped Pocahontas. She was 17 years old. By the age of 20, her name, religion and way of life had changed, and she was a wife and a mother. She lived in London, England, and was the honoured guest of royal parties.

The **settlers** kidnapped Pocahontas because they wanted Chief Powhatan to give them corn. They also wanted him to release English prisoners and goods taken by his warriors during battles.

▼ After Pocahontas was kidnapped, some women settlers taught her English customs, such as wearing dresses, **petticoats** and leather shoes.

Pocahontas's last years
Spring, 1613 she is kidnapped by the English
Summer, 1613 she learns about Christianity and is baptized with a new name, Rebecca
Spring, 1614 she marries John Rolfe, a tobacco farmer
Spring, 1615 she gives birth to a son, Thomas
Spring, 1616 John Rolfe, Pocahontas, and Thomas sail for London, England
Spring, 1617 she falls ill with smallpox and dies in England

A new home and a new identity

Chief Powhatan sent spies to check on Pocahontas. She was healthy and well cared for, they said. So Powhatan would not make a deal with the English. He did not trust them. Soon after, Pocahontas was taken to a new **settlement** called Henrico. There she stayed with Reverend Alexander Whitaker. Soon she was going to church and memorizing prayers. Eventually she was **baptized** with the Christian name, Rebecca.

Marriage to John Rolfe

John Rolfe came to Virginia in 1610 to grow tobacco. The Indians already grew tobacco, but Rolfe created a new, good-tasting variety. This new crop helped many colonists and Rolfe become rich.

◀ Pocahontas, now called Rebecca, sails from Virginia with her husband, son, sister and about 12 other Native Americans.

▼ A portrait of Pocahontas dressed as an English lady. It was painted in 1616 by an unknown English artist.

▶ This is a statue of Pocahontas at the Jamestown site. In March 1617, she, John and Thomas began their trip back to Virginia. Barely out of London, Pocahontas became ill with smallpox and soon died. She was buried in the town of Gravesend in Kent. John went back to Virginia. Thomas was educated in England, then returned to America.

Rolfe met Pocahontas at church. When he asked her to marry him, she agreed. In the spring of 1614, they were married. A year later, their son was born. Chief Powhatan seemed happy about this marriage. For a while, there was peace between the Powhatan and the colonists.

Pocahontas travels to England

The colonial leaders wanted support from England and to sell tobacco there. So, on 12 June 1616, Rolfe took Pocahontas, their son and a small group of other Powhatans to London. Rich people and royalty in London invited Pocahontas to many parties. She was astonished by the city. It was busy and filled with horses, carriages and clanging church bells. After spending seven months in London, Pocahontas wanted to return to Virginia.

Pocahontas heard that John Smith was living in London. She looked for him wherever she went. Finally he came to see her. Pocahontas was too hurt to be friendly. She spoke angrily to him. They never saw each other again. Pocahontas died in 1617 on her way back to America.

1619 to 1622

Virginia Plantations

Forget about finding gold! Virginia colonists were going to get rich by growing tobacco and selling it in England. Each year, hundreds of new colonists arrived in Virginia. New settlements sprang up outside Jamestown. People planted tobacco seeds everywhere – even in the streets and graveyards.

◀ On 22 March 1622, the Native Americans, led by Pocahontas's uncle, attacked and killed about 350 colonists in Jamestown. Many Native Americans were killed or **enslaved** by the English. The fighting continued for many years. This 1634 **engraving** by Theodore De Bry shows the battle.

▲ Each tobacco plant required lots of land. The colonists chopped down areas of forests to make tobacco fields. The Native Americans were furious about this.

▼ The colonists brought people from Africa to work on the plantations. As servants, they had to work for their keep.

Serious tobacco planters needed large farms and many workers. The large farms were called **plantations**. At first, the **colonists** used Native Americans as workers. But many Native Americans were dying of diseases brought from England – even trifling illnesses such as the common cold. Others ran away. In 1619, a ship arrived in Jamestown with Africans aboard. They had been taken away from their country to be sold as **servants**. After working several years they were meant to be free. By the late 1600s, most of the Africans in Virginia were **slaves**. They had no hope of freedom.

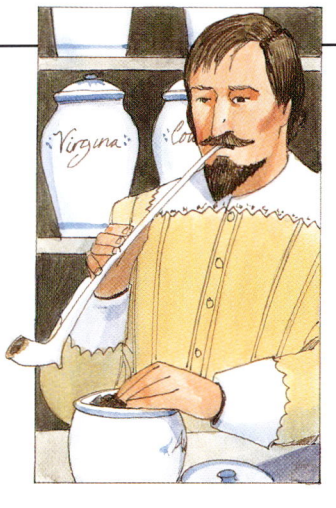

▲ In late August, tobacco plants were cut and hung upside down in a barn. After several months, the dried leaves were shipped to England.

▲ John Rolfe sent new flavourful blends of smoking tobacco to England, and the people loved it. It was the **colony**'s first money-making crop.

The growing colony
Many people from England packed their belongings and sailed for Virginia. All their lives they dreamed of owning land. In America it could happen. Until now, the Virginia Company of London had owned all the land. Now it was offering 20 hectares of land to anyone who paid their own passage by ship from England.

In 1619, Virginia started to become a family colony. That year, a ship arrived with 90 brave women from England. They had answered an advertisement. The Virginia colony wanted single women who were looking for husbands.

Not everyone in Virginia lived on large plantations. Most people lived in small cottages with small gardens. They grew only enough food to feed their families.

▼ In 1619, the Virginia Company gave the colonists the right to make some of their own laws. The free males in the colony elected a total of 22 **representatives,** called burgesses. These people formed the House of Burgesses. They made laws about trading with the Native Americans. They also set prices on tobacco. This modern painting of the House of Burgesses was made by Jack Clifton.

1620 to 1622

The Mayflower Arrives

"They now had no friends to welcome them nor inns to refresh their weatherbeaten bodies. Behind them, there was a mighty ocean to separate them from all the civil parts of the world." This is how William Bradford, governor of Plymouth Colony, described the Pilgrims who arrived there in the winter of 1620.

Why would anyone leave a nice village in England to venture into an unknown wilderness? Many people went to America for religious freedom. Everyone in England was supposed to belong to the same Protestant Church, which later became known as the Church of England. One group, called Puritans, did not like all the **rituals** of this church. They wanted to purify the religion by making services simpler and studying more of the Bible.

A number of Puritans wanted to separate from the Protestant Church. Because this was a serious crime, they decided to go to America. Their voyage took 66 days. They landed at Plymouth.

▼ A wintery scene at the reconstruction of Plymouth Plantation in Massachusetts. Many of the Pilgrims' houses have been recreated.

▲ Everyday life at Plymouth was very simple. Food was often cooked outdoors on an open fire. Children helped their parents.

◄ The first group of Puritans to leave England sailed to America on the *Mayflower*, a 27-m-long ship. It carried 102 passengers to Massachusetts. This painting, by Tompkins Matteson, shows the signing of the *Mayflower Compact* on the ship. The first Puritans to go to America later became known as the Pilgrims.

Plymouth Rock
The *Mayflower* was supposed to land near Jamestown, but the seas were too rough. Fearing a shipwreck, the ship landed in Cape Cod, Massachusetts, on 19 November 1620.

The group's leaders, John Carver and William Bradford, picked a site for their **colony.** A map made by John Smith called the place Plimoth (Plymouth). On 21 December, they brought the Pilgrims there. Plymouth Rock marks their landing spot, though no one is sure if this is accurate.

◀ The passengers and crew of The *Mayflower* unload the ship at Plymouth.

The *Mayflower Compact*

The Pilgrims wrote some rules to help people get along with each other. This document is called the *Mayflower Compact*. The people promised to "join together in a civill body politick... for the generall good of ye Colonie". This was the first agreement for **self-government** in the country. Although freedom was important to the Pilgrims, they were willing to have laws so they could live together peacefully.

Thanksgiving

In the spring, Native Americans of the Wampanoag **tribe** taught the Pilgrims how to plant corn and where to catch fish. Next autumn, after a good harvest, the Pilgrims invited around 90 Wampanoag to the first Thanksgiving feast.

1640 to 1680

A Home In The Colonies

News travelled back to the Puritans in England. Massachusetts was a safe place for Puritans to practise their religion. Starting in 1630, thousands of Puritans settled in Salem, Boston and other towns. They were all part of the Massachusetts Bay Colony.

▼ Settlers brought with them many things from England. This wine glass and leather tankard for drinking ale were found at the Plymouth site.

When new **settlers** arrived, they had to quickly build a shelter. Usually they built a tent covered with sail cloth. At other times they dug a cave into the hillside.

After crops were planted, the settlers built real houses. They first built one-room cottages with fireplaces. By 1640, they built larger, more comfortable homes. Building a house was a big job. A settler had to cut the trees, shape the logs, fit them together and gather stones for a cellar and chimney.

▲ This illustration, from a book published in the United States in 1853, shows the typical clothing of a Pilgrim man and woman from Plymouth **Colony**.

Keeping the fire burning

The fireplace was the most important part of the house. The meals were cooked in a hanging pot over the fire. The fire also provided heat and light. There were no matches, so settlers had to strike sparks from flint and steel. They tried to keep a fire burning all year round. If a fire went out, a child went to a neighbour and borrowed a few hot coals to get it started again.

Eating – sitting or standing

At mealtimes, the men and older boys sat at the table to eat. If there was a servant or daughter to bring in the food, the wife sat beside her husband. Young children ate while standing silently by the table.

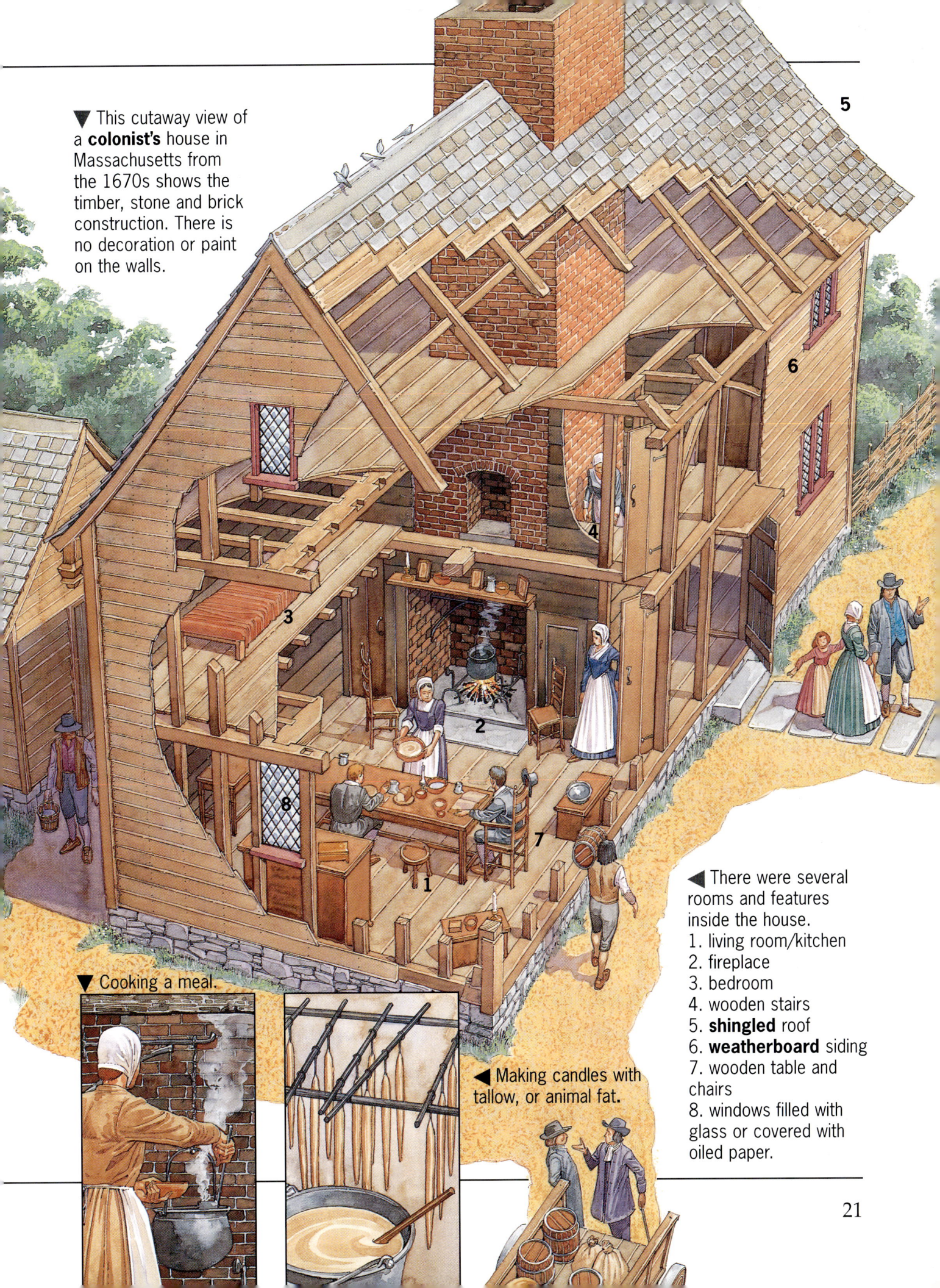

▼ This cutaway view of a **colonist's** house in Massachusetts from the 1670s shows the timber, stone and brick construction. There is no decoration or paint on the walls.

◀ There were several rooms and features inside the house.
1. living room/kitchen
2. fireplace
3. bedroom
4. wooden stairs
5. **shingled** roof
6. **weatherboard** siding
7. wooden table and chairs
8. windows filled with glass or covered with oiled paper.

▼ Cooking a meal.

◀ Making candles with tallow, or animal fat.

21

1630 to 1680

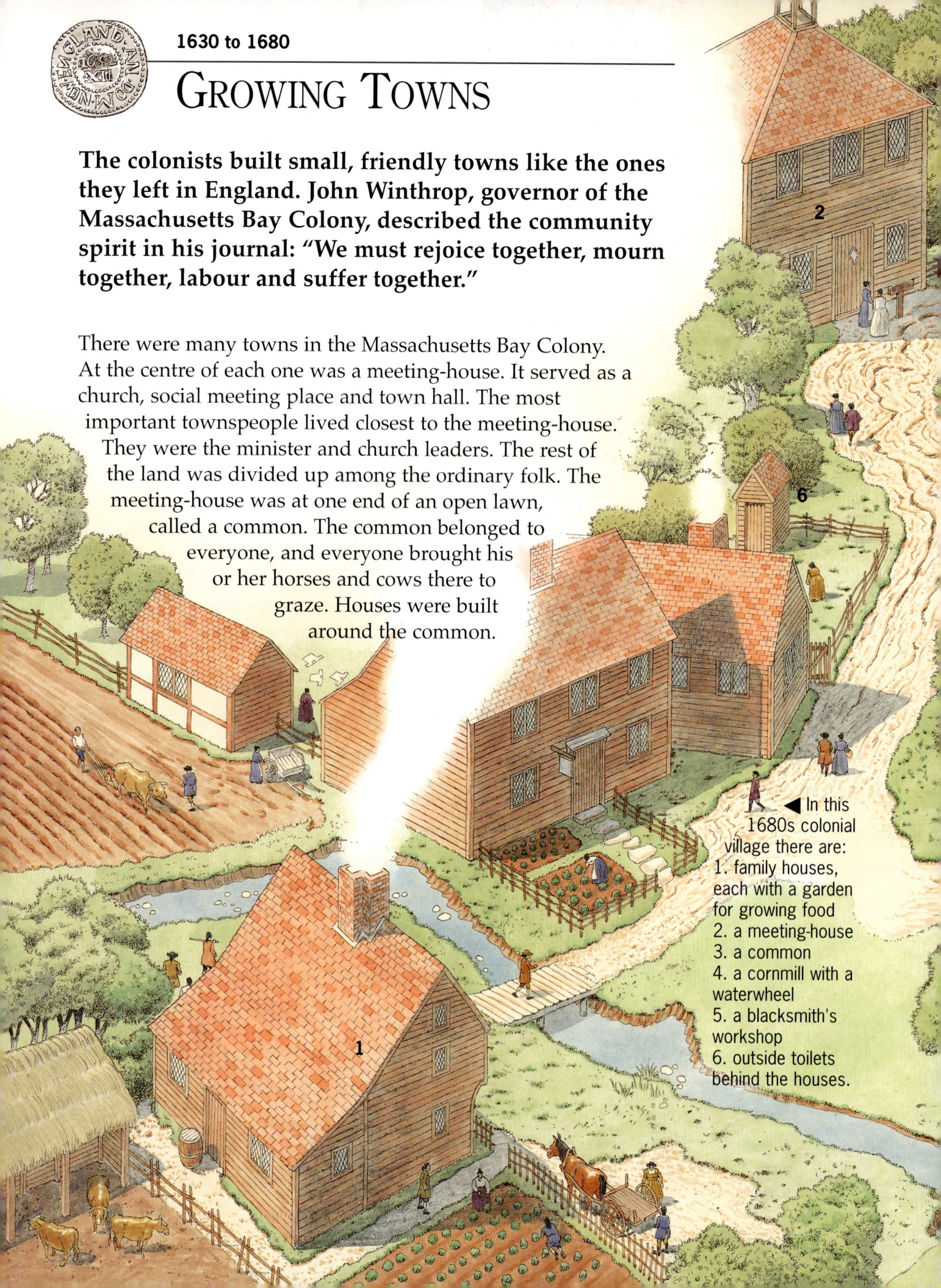

GROWING TOWNS

The colonists built small, friendly towns like the ones they left in England. John Winthrop, governor of the Massachusetts Bay Colony, described the community spirit in his journal: "We must rejoice together, mourn together, labour and suffer together."

There were many towns in the Massachusetts Bay Colony. At the centre of each one was a meeting-house. It served as a church, social meeting place and town hall. The most important townspeople lived closest to the meeting-house. They were the minister and church leaders. The rest of the land was divided up among the ordinary folk. The meeting-house was at one end of an open lawn, called a common. The common belonged to everyone, and everyone brought his or her horses and cows there to graze. Houses were built around the common.

◀ In this 1680s colonial village there are:
1. family houses, each with a garden for growing food
2. a meeting-house
3. a common
4. a cornmill with a waterwheel
5. a blacksmith's workshop
6. outside toilets behind the houses.

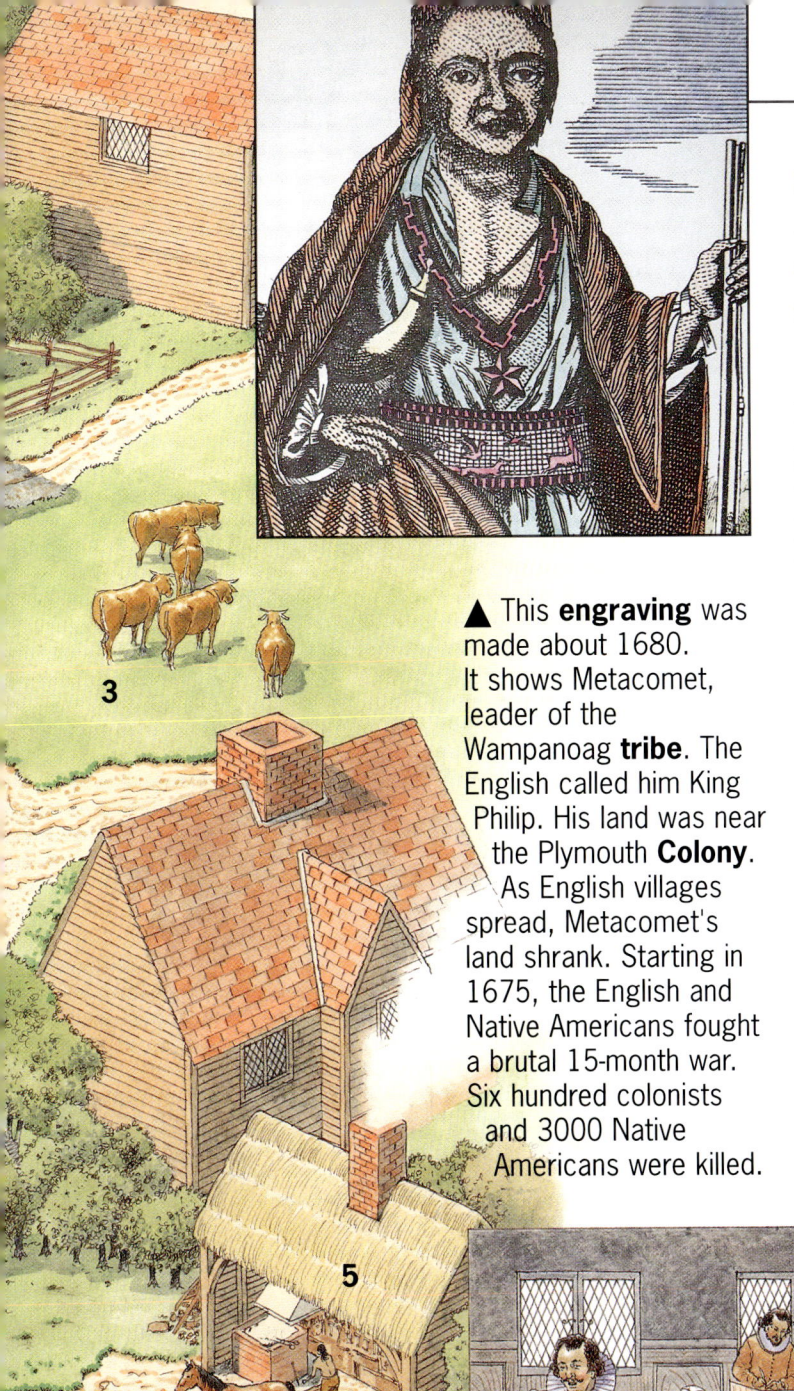

Shops and schools

As a town grew, people opened up shops and stores. There was usually a general store, a blacksmith's and a candle shop.

Almost every town built a school. Education was important to the Puritans. In 1642, the Massachusetts Bay Colony passed a law that all parents must teach their children to read the Bible. By 1647, a law stated that every town with 50 or more families had to hire a professional teacher to teach the children to read and write. Children spent up to ten hours a day in school.

Church

Everyone had to go to church on Sunday. The minister's sermon could last for hours. After the service, people met in the churchyard to exchange views. There were many rules about Sundays. No working, playing or cooking was allowed. It was strictly a day of rest.

▲ This **engraving** was made about 1680. It shows Metacomet, leader of the Wampanoag **tribe**. The English called him King Philip. His land was near the Plymouth **Colony**. As English villages spread, Metacomet's land shrank. Starting in 1675, the English and Native Americans fought a brutal 15-month war. Six hundred colonists and 3000 Native Americans were killed.

▲ Many decisions were made at town meetings. Every man could vote, as long as he owned property and was a church member. Men voted for town officers, new teachers and ways to raise money for buildings and the upkeep of the town.

▼ In school, each child had a hornbook. This was a flat piece of wood with a cover of animal horn made clear by boiling it. Papers to read were placed under the cover to protect them.

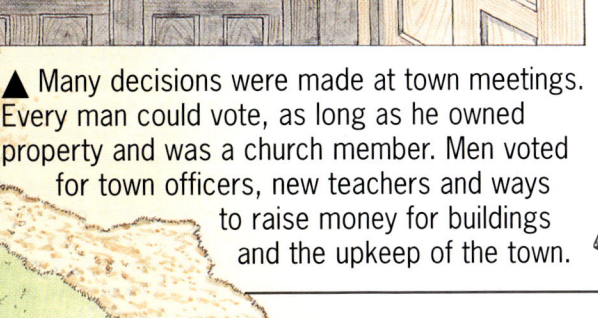

1609 to 1664
NEW NETHERLANDS

The year was 1609. Native Americans were living on Manhattan Island, which is today part of New York City. They probably were shocked to see a big ship sail by on its way up the river. An English explorer, Henry Hudson, sailed the ship. The Netherlands had hired him to claim land in North America.

According to legend, in 1626 the **Dutch** bought Manhattan Island from the Carnarsee Native Americans for beads and other things worth $24. The Dutch founded New Amsterdam in the **colony** of New Netherlands. For a while, the Dutch and the Native Americans lived peacefully together. The Dutch opened **trading posts**. Native Americans trapped beavers and brought the furs to the trading posts. Merchants bought the furs and made beaver hats out of them. People in Europe paid a lot of money for beaver hats because they were fashionable and rare there.

New York's timeline
1524 Verrazano sails up New York harbour as he explores the coast
1609 Henry Hudson reaches Manhattan Island
1624 the Dutch start settling in New Netherlands, which includes present-day New York, New Jersey and several nearby states
1626 the Dutch purchase Manhattan Island and start the town of New Amsterdam (today's New York City)
1664 the English take over New Netherlands and rename it New York
1664 New Jersey becomes a separate colony

▼ By 1660, about 1000 people with various religions and languages lived in New Amsterdam. Located on a **harbour,** it became a bustling sailors' town.

▼ People and goods arrived at New Amsterdam harbour from all over the world. The warehouses, houses and bridges in the harbour were built in the Dutch style. There were also Dutch windmills for grinding corn.

▲ Peter Stuyvesant was the last Dutch governor of New Netherlands. He was an unpopular leader. In 1664, English ships came to take over the colony. Stuyvesant had neither enough guns nor Dutch people to help him fight. He surrendered and the English took over.

The English take over

The English wanted to own New Netherlands. They already owned Massachusetts to the north and Virginia to the south. The English arrived in 1664. Most Dutch people did not care to fight. After the English took over, they allowed the Dutch people to stay in their villages and practise their religions. The loss of New Netherlands was a cause of the Dutch–English wars in Europe in 1665.

New York and New Jersey

England's King Charles II put his brother, the Duke of York, in charge of his new colony. Right away, the duke changed the colony's name to New York. Soon he gave some of the colony to his friends, Sir George Carteret and Lord John Berkeley. They named their land New Jersey, after the island in the English Channel.

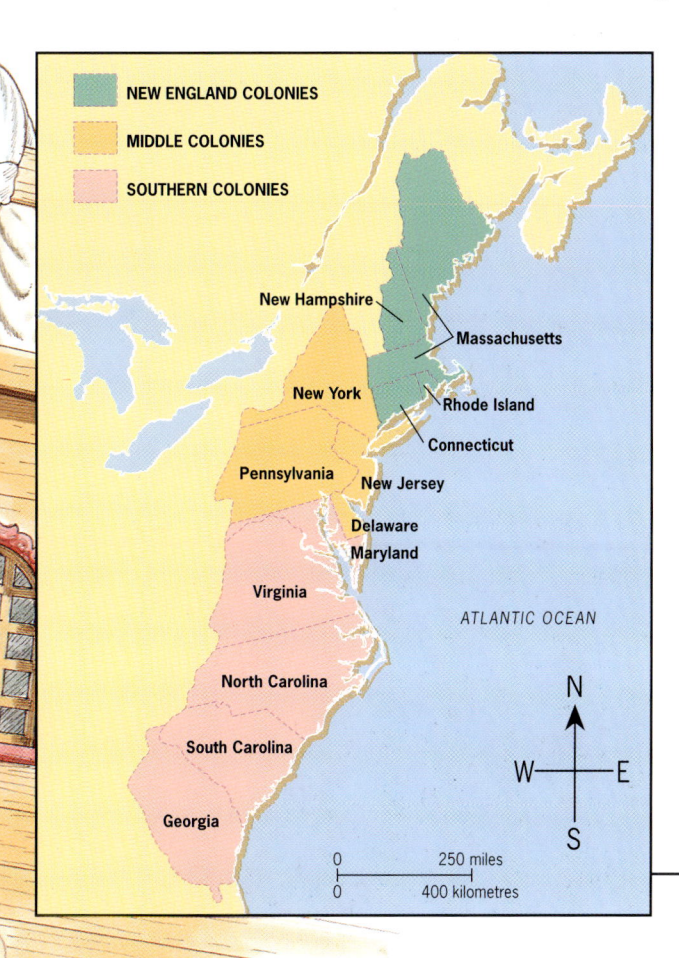

- NEW ENGLAND COLONIES
- MIDDLE COLONIES
- SOUTHERN COLONIES

◀ This map shows the English colonies. By 1733, there were 13. These colonies became the first United States of America.

When the colonies started:
1607 Virginia
1620 Massachusetts
1623 New Hampshire
1624 New York
1633 Connecticut
1634 Maryland
1636 Rhode Island
1638 Delaware
1643 Pennsylvania
1653 North Carolina
1660 New Jersey
1670 South Carolina
1733 Georgia.

1603 to 1683

NEW FRANCE

The English colonies took up only a tiny part of North America. What was north and west of the colonies? Were there mountains, rivers, people? How far did the land stretch? Explorers from France wanted to answer these questions. They paddled canoes up rivers and along the shores of lakes.

▼ In 1682, Robert La Salle and his crew travelled the Mississippi River from Montreal in Canada all the way to the Gulf of Mexico. During the two-month voyage, they built forts, **claimed** land and passed many Native American villages. Some Native Americans attacked them. Others were friendly and offered them food and advice.

▲ One huge obstacle in La Salle's route was Niagara Falls, between Lakes Erie and Ontario. La Salle and the others carried their canoes around the falls.

▲ Near the Arkansas River, La Salle raised a Christian cross in front of Native Americans of the Quapaw **tribe** to claim the surrounding land for France.

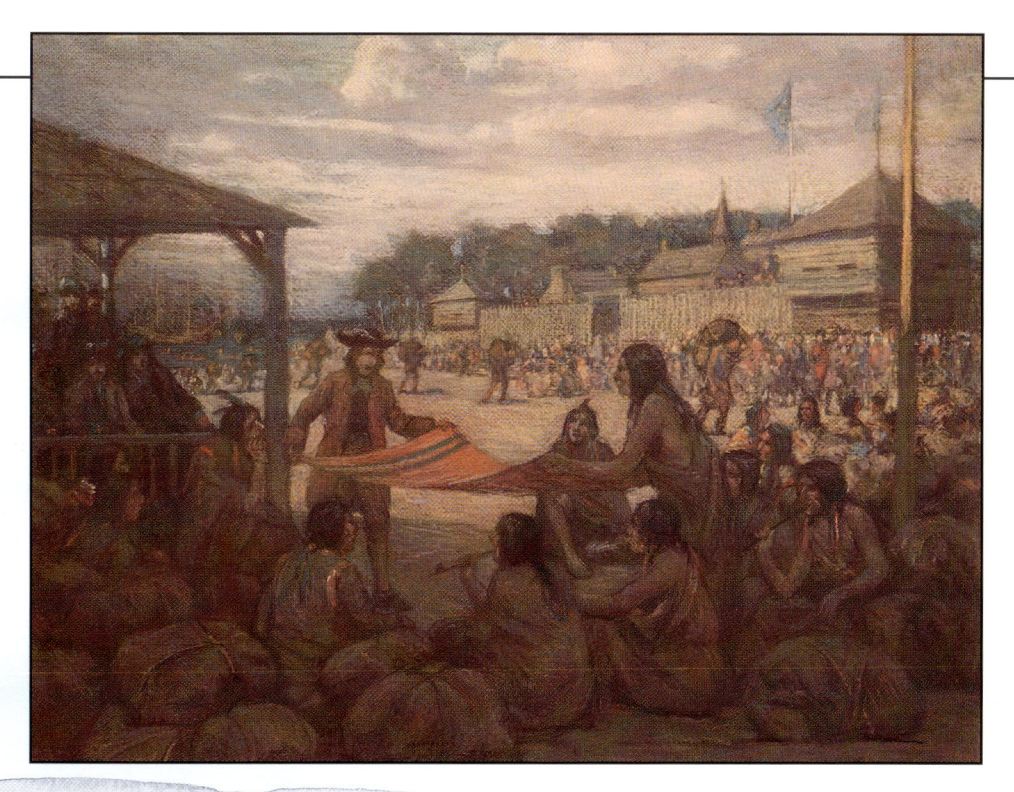

French fur traders exchange sacks of beaver furs for blankets with Native Americans at Montreal, in a 1900s painting by George Reid.

French explorers travelled the St Lawrence River, the Great Lakes and the Mississippi River. They were disappointed to find out that these waterways did not lead to the Pacific Ocean. The explorers travelled on foot and in canoes.

The French explorer Samuel de Champlain started to explore the St Lawrence River in 1603. He spent 30 years paddling through what is now Canada. He had two goals. First, he was trying to find the water passageway from the Atlantic to the Pacific Oceans. Second, he wanted to build French **trading posts** throughout Canada. In 1608, he started the first permanent **settlement** in New France, at Quebec.

Claiming land for France

In 1673, Father Jacques Marquette, a French Jesuit priest, and Louis Joliet, a French fur trapper, paddled through the St Lawrence River and the Great Lakes to the Mississippi River.

Robert La Salle followed the Mississippi River even further south. He went to the Gulf of Mexico in 1682. La Salle claimed all the land along the Mississippi River for France. He named it Louisiana, in honour of France's King Louis XIV.

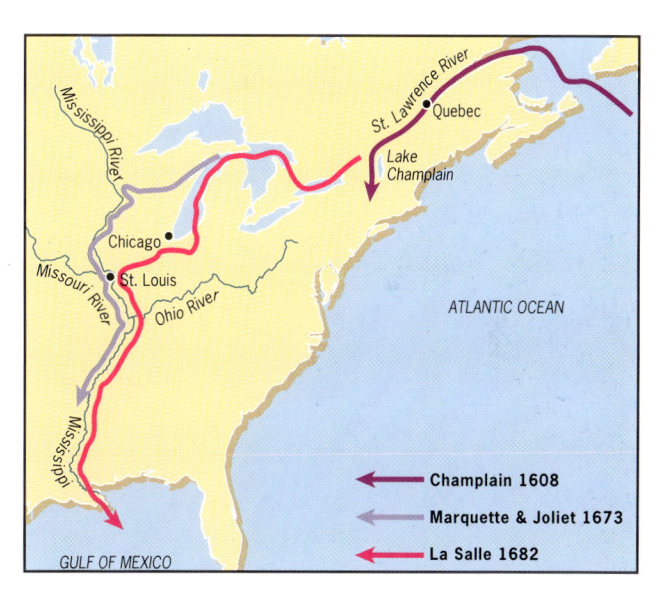

The French built their settlements by rivers and the Great Lakes. At each settlement, they first built a fort for protection. Then they built houses for their soldiers and **settlers.** They cleared land for farms and built a mill to grind wheat and maize into flour. Most settlements were fur-trading centres. Native Americans came to trade furs for French goods. These settlements grew into cities, such as Chicago and St Louis.

1680s to 1700s

West of the Colonies

As French and English settlers moved westward, they chased away the Native Americans. Many eastern tribes ended up in the Great Plains. Some tribes fought each other. Others worked together.

The land west of the Mississippi was still Native American country. These **tribes** may have heard stories about 'white men'. Most had never seen one. Many of these tribes farmed the land, growing corn, beans and pumpkins. They also hunted deer, rabbits and birds, and gathered wild fruits and vegetables.

On the northern **Great Plains,** Native Americans lived in earth lodges built on the banks of the Missouri River. Those of the Western Plains lived in portable homes, called tepees. Each summer, they packed up their tepees and followed the buffalo herds. By the 1600s, there were wild horses on the Great Plains. Some of these horses had escaped from Spanish **settlers** in Mexico. Others had been stolen from the Spaniards.

▲ This is the word 'No' in Native American sign language. It was developed in the Great Plains so that tribes that had never met before could talk together.

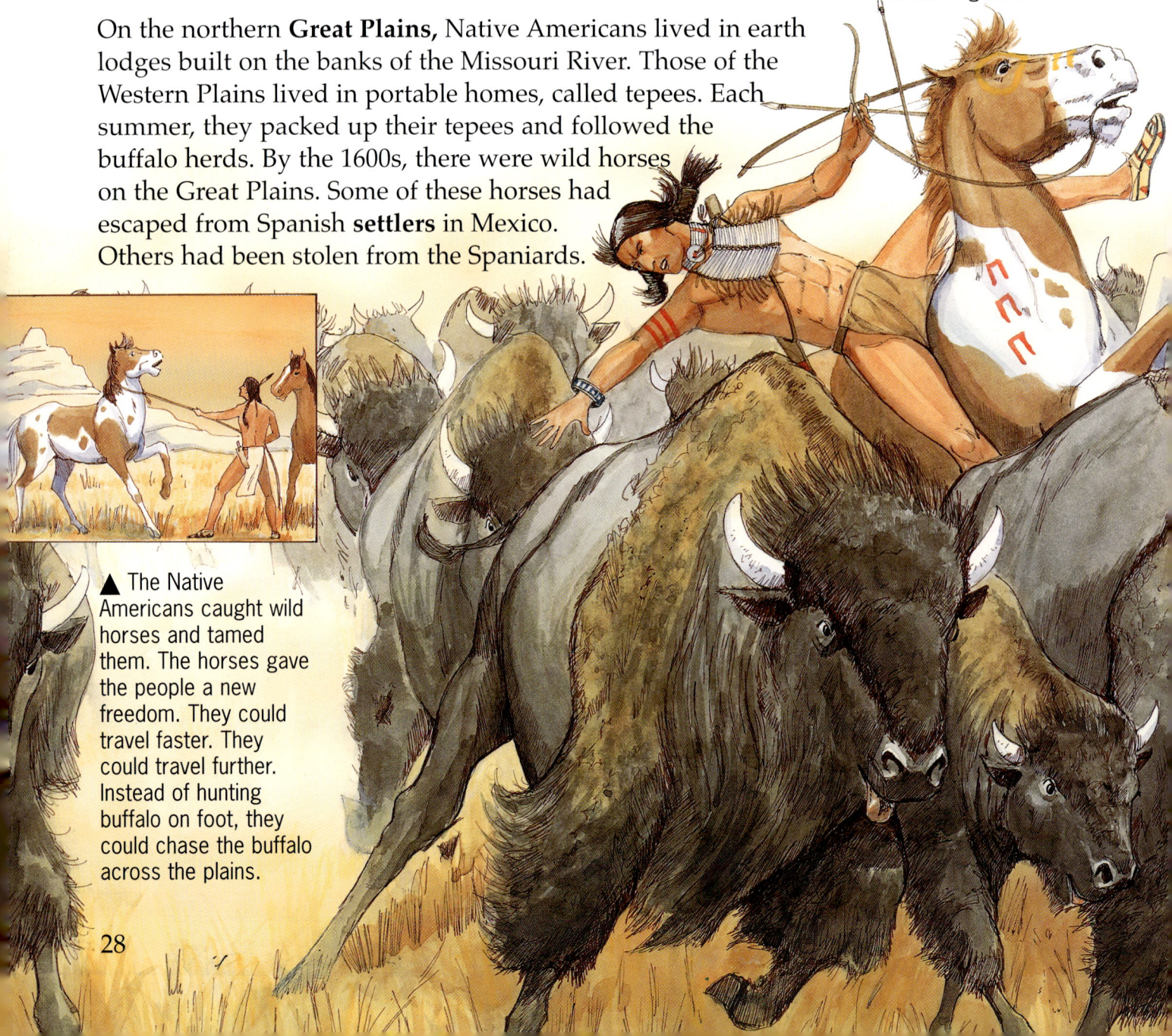

▲ The Native Americans caught wild horses and tamed them. The horses gave the people a new freedom. They could travel faster. They could travel further. Instead of hunting buffalo on foot, they could chase the buffalo across the plains.

The buffalo hunt

Millions of buffalo roamed the Great Plains. Now that the Native Americans had horses, they could follow the herds for great distances. Sometimes Native Americans would build a corral, or fenced-in area. Then a large group of riders would chase a herd, shouting and waving brightly coloured robes. They would chase the buffalo into the corral, then shoot them with bows and arrows.

▼ These Assiniboine could pack up their village in a few hours. Tepees and belongings were strapped onto poles and carried by horses. The people travelled on foot and on horseback.

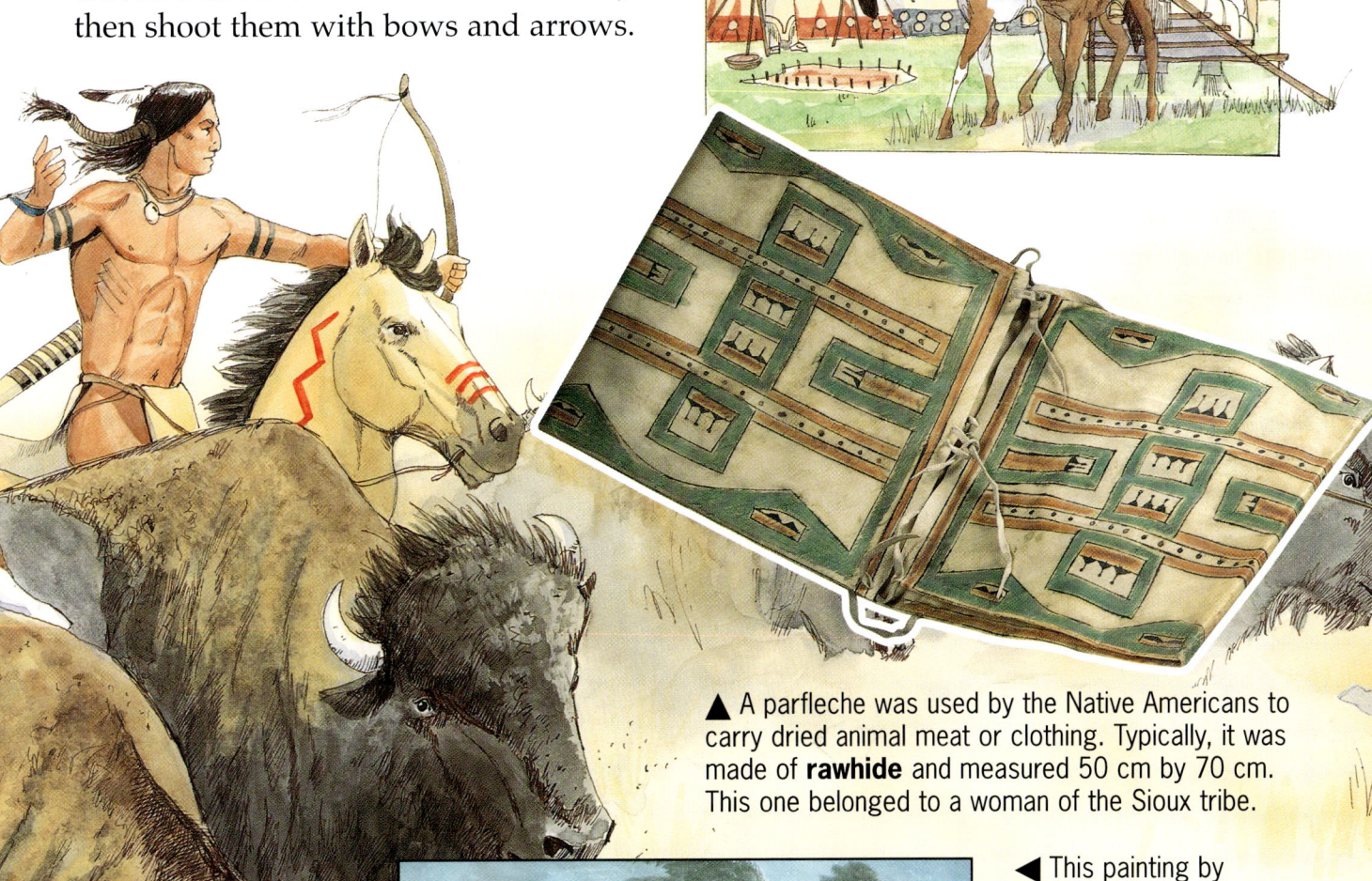

▲ A parfleche was used by the Native Americans to carry dried animal meat or clothing. Typically, it was made of **rawhide** and measured 50 cm by 70 cm. This one belonged to a woman of the Sioux tribe.

◀ This painting by George Catlin shows a Sioux tepee villlage. Tepees were made bigger once horses were available to pull heavy loads. In the middle of the tepee, the Native Americans made a fire for cooking and warmth. They slept on buffalo skins or willow mats.

1598 to late 1700s

MISSIONS IN THE WEST

Along with European explorers came the missionaries. They were priests. Their job was to persuade the Native Americans to become Christians. In Florida and California, the Spanish and French governments built many missions. They brought Native Americans there to live, work and learn how to be loyal Spanish and French citizens.

"You say that you are sent to instruct us how to worship the Great Spirit, and if we do not take hold of the religion which you white people teach, we shall be unhappy hereafter. You say you are right and we are lost. How do we know this to be true? We also have a religion which was given to our forefathers...." These were the words of an Iroquois leader named Red Jacket. It was his answer to French **missionaries** on the East Coast who wanted to change his religion.

Spanish missions

There were many Spanish **missions** in California. A mission was a small farm built around a church. Native Americans did most of the building and most of the farming. In exchange, they were given food, homes and protection from their enemies. They were taught to read and write (in Spanish). They were taught how to become Catholic Christians.

At first, many Native Americans welcomed the comforts of mission life. Later, many resented it. They were no longer free to do as they pleased. They resented having their customs, traditions and beliefs attacked.

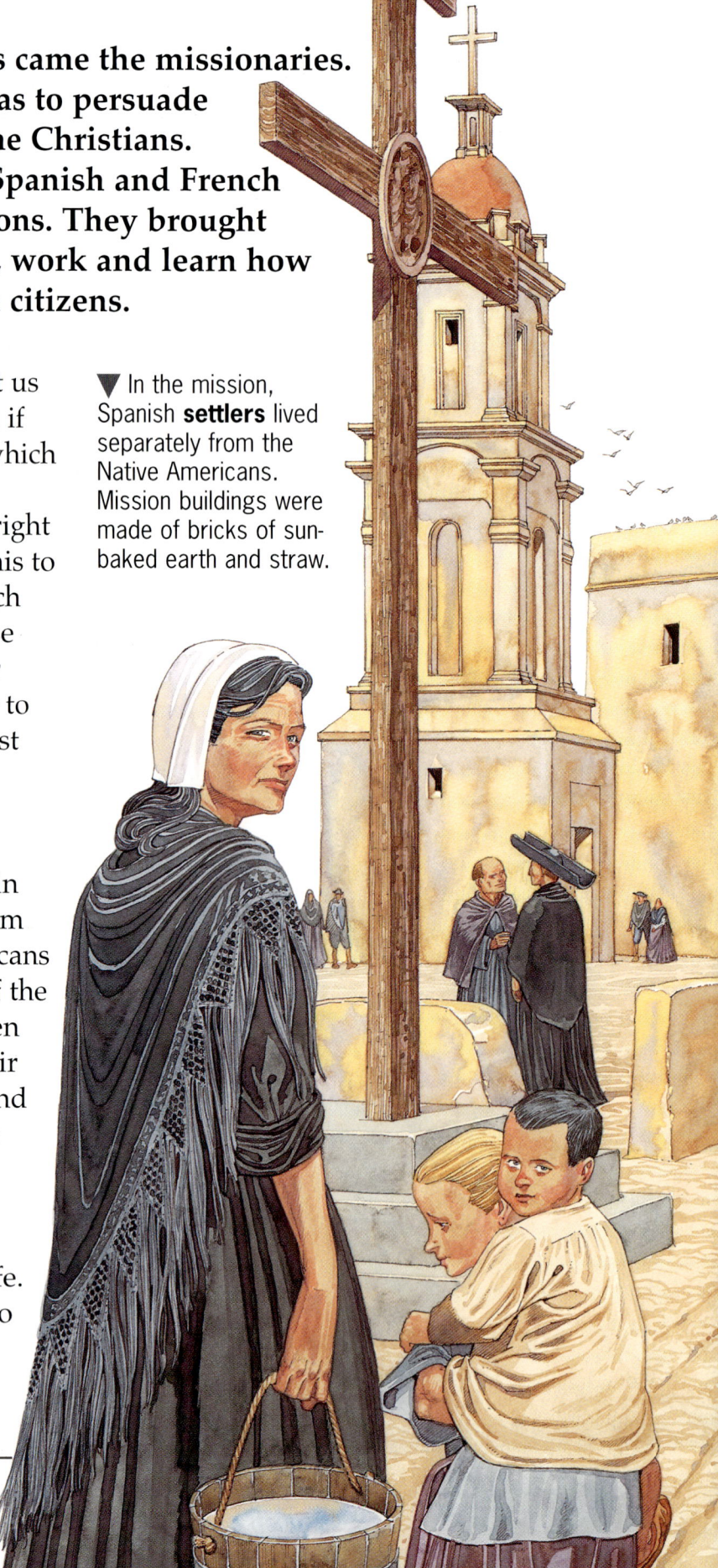

▼ In the mission, Spanish **settlers** lived separately from the Native Americans. Mission buildings were made of bricks of sun-baked earth and straw.

30

▲ Native Americans dance outside San Francisco mission, in a painting by M. Louis Choris from 1813.

▼ Most mission buildings were set around open courtyards, as shown in the inset below left. Most Spanish missions had these features:
• a church
• corrals for raising horses, cows and sheep
• fields for growing grains and vegetables
• a dining area
• a school
• living areas
• workshops to teach carpentry and metalwork.

◀ This is the bell tower at San Diego Mission in California. Each morning, the Native Americans went to Catholic church services and took lessons in the religion. San Diego Mission was built in 1769.

31

1700 to 1750

THE SHOPS OF BOSTON

By 1750, Boston had 20,000 people. It was one of the most important cities in the colonies. Wealthy Bostonians rode in horse-drawn carriages, but most people walked down Boston's cobblestone streets. Welcoming signs hung outside the shops of shoemakers, bakers, carpenters and tailors.

Colonial craftworkers were proud of their work. Some learned their craft from their parents. Others had been young **apprentices,** living and working with a skilled craftworker. People rarely used money to buy things. Instead, they bartered, or traded. A tailor might barter a wool jacket for a pair of leather shoes.

▼ This 'pine tree shilling' coin was made by colonists in 1652. People also used money from France, Spain and England.

A tailor

◄► Shopping was different from today. People could not look through racks of clothes or shoes to find something they liked. Instead, tailors measured people and made them jackets or dresses. Shoemakers did the same thing. Carpenters built furniture, copying the styles of England.

A carpenter

A shoemaker

Both men and women worked in the shops. Jobs were specialized. That means a person made only one thing. There was a brickmaker, a wigmaker, a saddle maker. There was the blacksmith who made horseshoes and tools out of iron, and the silversmith who made fancy things out of silver. There was a chandler who made candles, and a sawyer who sawed wood.

Rich and poor together
Boston's rich people lived in large brick houses with servants. They often imported fine cloth or finished clothing from Europe. Poor people lived in crowded wooden buildings and moved around looking for jobs. Many poor women earned money by taking in other people's laundry and sewing. Most shopkeepers were wealthy but not rich.

▶ A coloured **engraving** of Boston in about 1730 by William Burgis.

▼ Craftworkers had workshops, such as this silversmith's shop. This woman may have had the silversmith melt down some silver coins to make a coffee pot. Silverware was a sign of wealth.

By 1700, Boston was America's centre of shipping, fishing and trade. English ships arrived in its harbour, carrying tea and sugar. Massachusetts' ships left for England with American timber.

In 1704, Boston had the first successful colonial newspaper, the *Boston News-Letter*.

1700 to 1735

GETTING THINGS DONE

"Little strokes fell big oaks," said Benjamin Franklin, a leading citizen of Philadelphia. In other words: big things get done in small steps. In colonial days, people did things differently from the way we do them today. Their way took longer than our way. Still, they were making progress.

In colonial days, there were no factories or computers to speed things up. Things got done in their own time. For example, at first, the mail was delivered without a schedule by passing travellers. By 1700, a special post rider rode from town to town, dropping off letters at inns and taverns. As the sun went down, people lighted oil lamps or candles to light their homes. Some cities had lights on the streets. People hung out lanterns and lamps at sundown, when a watchman called to them: "Hang out your lights."

▶ This is Ben Franklin's print shop. His newspaper, the *Pennsylvania Gazette*, was famous all over the colonies. He published it from 1729 to 1766. His inventions included:
- stoves that made more heat with less fuel
- the first ever lightning conductor
- bifocal eyeglasses that helped people see close up and at a distance
- lending libraries, which allowed people to read books without paying for them
- a postal service with speedier delivery times.

▲ Clockmakers made the 'insides' of clocks. Sometimes people hung the clocks on a wall. If they could afford it, they went to a carpenter and had a wooden case made for the insides of a clock.

▲ The glassmaker took a mixture of flint, soda and lead and placed it in a roaring fire. When the mixture heated to a liquid, it was put on a blowpipe. The glassblower shaped it into a bottle.

▲ For medicines, most people tried home cures. If they were very sick, they might go to a doctor. This painting from 1776 shows a doctor feeling the pulse of a person with smallpox. The patient is kept behind a curtain as a precaution, because the disease is easily passed on to others.

▼ From 1733 to 1758, Benjamin Franklin published *Poor Richard's Almanack*. It was filled with advice, jokes, weather predictions and witty sayings, such as "A penny saved is a penny earned". At first, Franklin used a **pen name,** Richard Saunders, when he wrote the book.

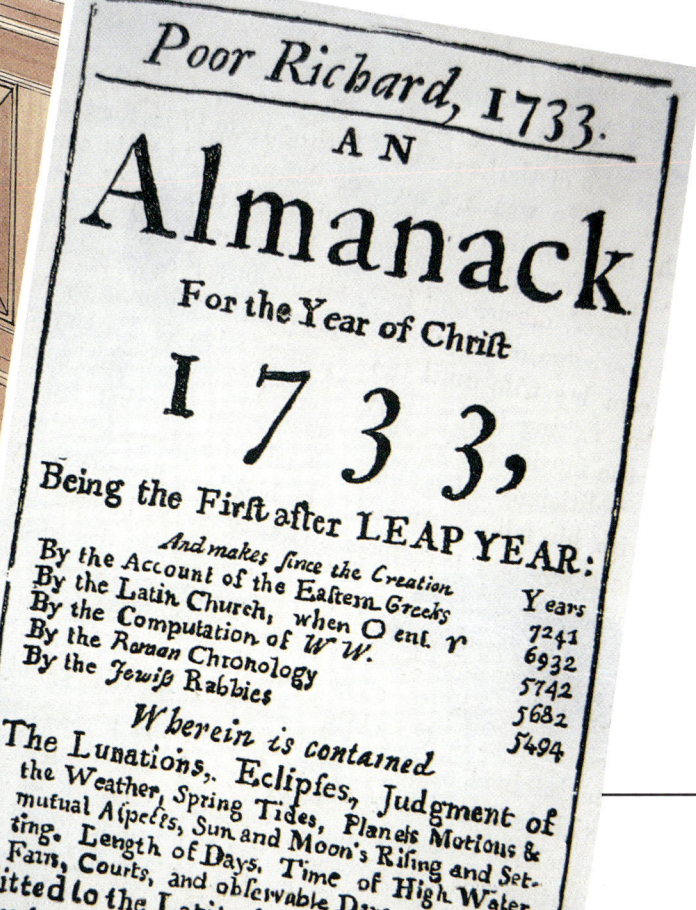

Telling the time

Early colonial clocks were large, inaccurate and most commonly seen on church towers. Most people told the time by looking at the position of the sun or listening for church bells. Some wealthy people owned grandfather clocks. By the mid-1700s, clocks were made smaller and more accurate. Still, buying a clock was an expensive investment.

Arts, medicine and better transport

The early 1700s saw the development of many new ideas. In 1716, the first theatre in the colonies was built in Williamsburg, Virginia. In 1721, America's first **vaccine** against smallpox was given in Boston. In 1732, the first regularly scheduled **stagecoach** line ran between Burlington and Amboy, New Jersey. From Burlington, passengers took a boat to Philadelphia. From Amboy, they took a boat to New York City.

1730 to 1750

Farming and Food

Nearly all colonists grew maize and wheat, enough to make bread for the family. They raised cows, chickens and pigs, which provided milk, eggs and meat. Some colonists had large farms and sold their extra crops to European merchants.

▼ This print of 1748 shows English ploughs imported to North America. Farmers were now using ploughs pulled by horses or oxen.

A farmer usually planted the same crop in the same part of his field, year after year. In time, the soil became poor. Then the farmer cleared a new area of land. By 1750, farmers understood how to use the land more wisely. They planted different crops each year. They also learned to use fertilizers to keep the soil rich.

When a new group of **immigrants** came to America, they introduced new kinds of fruits or vegetables. The **Dutch** brought water melons, spinach and parsley. Germans brought asparagus and cauliflower. People from Scotland and Ireland brought white potatoes.

A variety of foods

Most meals included American corn, or maize, in the form of either cornbread, corn mush or succotash – made with maize and beans. There were no refrigerators so **colonists smoked** and pickled their meats to keep them from spoiling. Lamb, chicken and turkey were available nearly everywhere.

Apple pie was probably invented in the colonies. A typical family sweetened its food with honey, molasses or maple sugar. The rich could afford European luxuries such as coffee, tea and chocolate.

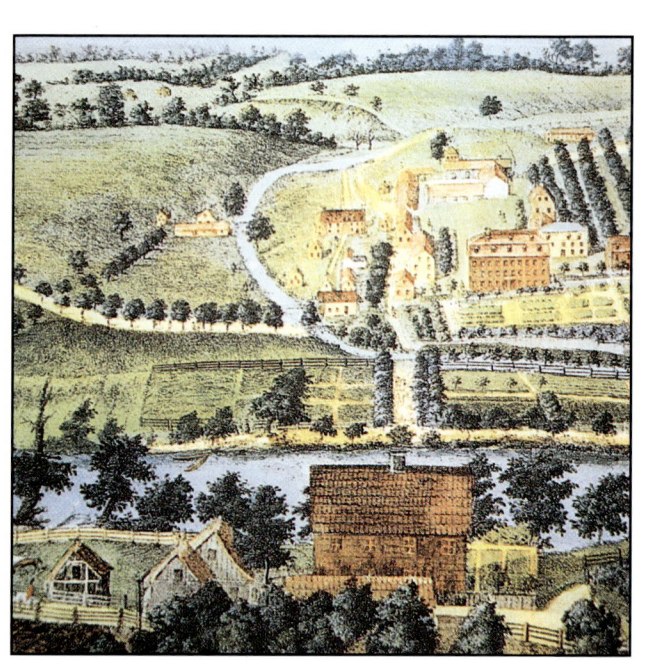

▲ This is Pennsylvania farmland in the 1750s. The entire family had responsibilities on the farm. Women and children helped turn the soil and get it ready for planting. They also collected eggs from the chickens and milk from the cows. It was the woman's job to churn the milk into butter.

36

▼ In wealthy people's houses, a dining room was used for special visitors and holiday meals. Until 1750, people used plain, steel forks to hold their meat while cutting it. It was acceptable to eat with your fingers. After 1750, eating with forks became fashionable. People began buying fancy silverware.

▲ Meat was hung over a smoky fire in a smoke house. Smoked ham was very popular.

▲ Fish, cucumbers and onions were pickled by soaking them in vinegar.

◀ A wealthy merchant would have several **servants** in his house. At mealtimes, the servants set the table and prepared the food.

Serving a hot meal in a large house was a challenge. Sometimes the kitchen was outside the house. By the time the food was carried to the dining room, it was cold. The servant might set it on a warming rack by the room's fire.

37

1730 to 1750

SLAVERY

"On a signal given, the buyers rush at once into the yard where the slaves are confined, and make choice of that parcel (person) they like best." An African man named Olaudah Equiano wrote how he was sold as a slave in the 1750s. His book was published in 1789.

Every day, **slave** ships sailed across the Atlantic Ocean. Each one carried hundreds of African men, women and children who had been torn away from their families and villages. The ships sailed from Africa to the **West Indies** or American **colonies** such as Virginia, Massachusetts and South Carolina. In the colonies, slave traders unloaded the slaves and reloaded the ships with American goods, such as tobacco, timber, **rum** and furs. The ships then headed for Europe, where these goods would be sold by merchants.

Plantation owners in the colonies were eager to buy slaves. They needed many workers in their large tobacco and rice fields. It was cheaper to purchase slaves than to pay people to do the work. They could also use 'undesirables' deported from Europe as unpaid workers. Some people in the colonies tried to stop slavery. Still, for many years, there were no laws against owning slaves or against owners treating their slaves horribly.

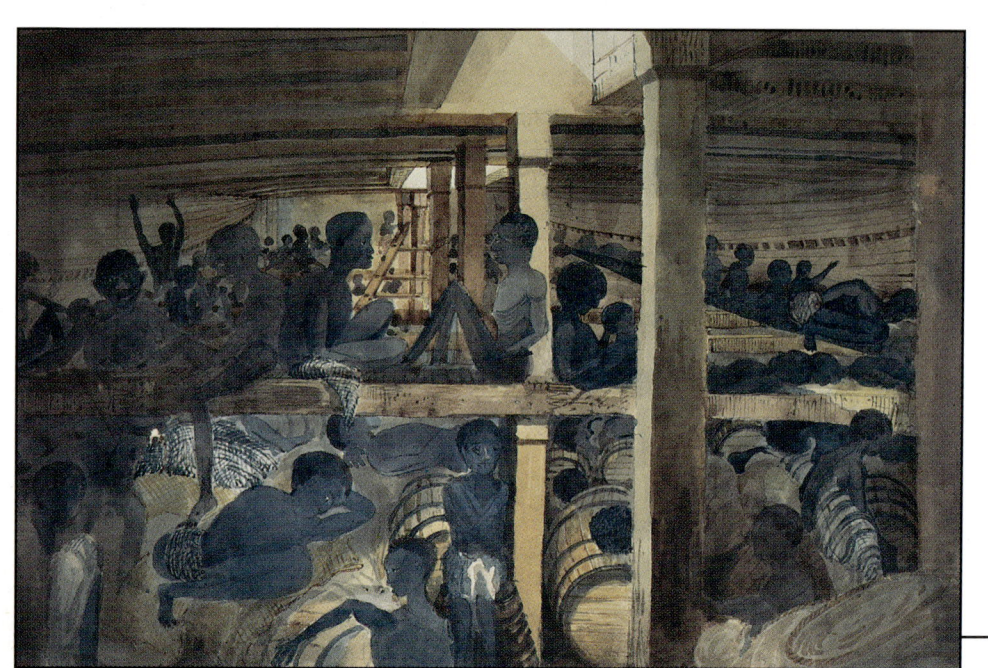

▲▼ Africans were taken and traded, as if they were of equal value to timber or rum. Triangle-shaped trading routes all involved slaves.

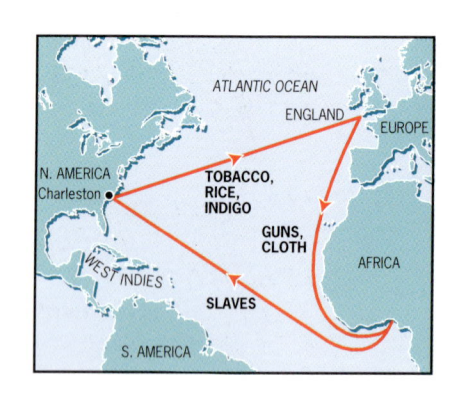

◀ An officer of an English slave ship painted this picture in the 1800s. His name was Daniel Henry Meynell. The ship was sailing from Africa to America. Officers crammed slaves together in all parts of the ship. Many slaves died of diseases in these filthy conditions. The rest were chained together. To them, their future was a horrifying mystery.

A slave's life

Most slaves worked on plantations. Most worked in the fields. Some cooked and cleaned in the master's house. Slaves had no freedom. They could not leave the plantation without permission. They could not learn to read and write. Many were whipped and treated cruelly.

Only when the slaves returned to their one-room cabins at night could they talk about the world they left behind. They would tell folk stories and play African music to keep their culture alive.

▶ At a slave auction, people shouted out a price they wanted to pay for a slave. The highest bidder won. People paid $1000 (about £19,000 at today's value) for a strong, skilled slave.

▼ This newspaper advertisement of 1766 announced a new arrival of African slaves in Charleston, South Carolina.

TO BE SOLD, on board the Ship *Bance-Island*, on tuesday the 6th of *May* next, at *Afhley-Ferry*; a choice cargo of about 250 fine healthy

NEGROES,

juſt arrived from the Windward & Rice Coaſt. —The utmoſt care has already been taken, and ſhall be continued, to keep them free from the leaſt danger of being infected with the SMALL-POX, no boat having been on board, and all other communication with people from *Charles-Town* prevented.

Auſtin, Laurens, & Appleby.

N. B. Full one Half of the above Negroes have had the SMALL-POX in their own Country.

1730 to 1754

CITY LIFE

"Keep thy shop and thy shop will keep thee." Benjamin Franklin wrote this in his almanac. He had all kinds of advice for his fellow citizens of Philadelphia. As the town was growing into America's largest city, Franklin came up with many ideas to make it safer and more pleasant.

▲ In colonial cities, most wealthy people wore fashionable clothes from England. Men's fashions included short trousers, called breeches, with stockings pulled over the knee. Women wore long dresses puffed out with **petticoats**.

◀ A street scene in Philadelphia in 1750.

Englishman William Penn, who was a devout Quaker, started the town of Philadelphia in 1682. Its name means 'brotherly love'. Penn promised freedom of religion to anyone who settled there. He drew plans for a 'greene countrie town', with broad, straight streets.

Thousands of people came from other **colonies** and many European countries to settle and enjoy life in Philadelphia. By 1730, it was a bustling city with shops, houses, schools, meeting-halls and dirt roads connecting it to other towns in Pennsylvania and New Jersey.

▼ In 1754, Ben Franklin met with **representatives** from seven colonies. He presented a Plan of Union. He wanted the colonies to work together to defend America and raise **taxes** independent of England. The plan was not approved until 1765.

40

▲ Children dressed like adults, but they still acted like children. In the countryside, girls joined the boys in spinning tops and pitching pennies. City girls played more quietly.

▲ Shopkeepers were called the 'middling sort' because they were neither rich nor poor. Women and men worked in family shops, selling such things as soap, shoes, candles and bread.

▲ Travellers came to do business in the city. They stayed with homeowners who rented out unused bedrooms. These places were called boarding houses and the guests lodgers.

▲ **Servants** and **slaves** were among the poorest people in the city. So were sailors and workers with temporary jobs. These people did not own property and were not allowed to vote.

Problem-solving and organizing

Along with progress came problems of city life. Carts, carriages and covered wagons stirred up dust and dug potholes. People collected unbearable amounts of rubbish in front of their houses. Crime on the dark streets was becoming a problem. Fires were destroying homes and shops.

Benjamin Franklin helped solve many of Philadelphia's problems. He worked to get the street sidewalks paved and to hire a lamplighter to fill and light the city streets' oil lamps. He worked to hire a 'scavenger', or street cleaner, to pick up the rubbish. He also helped organize a fire department, police department, city hospital, library, university and postal delivery service.

▲ This cartoon was published by Benjamin Franklin as tensions were growing between the colonies and England. It shows England as a woman having lost her four limbs: New York, New England, Pennsylvania and Virginia. Without her shield and spear, England is defenceless against the colonies.

41

1590 to 1754

Historical Map of America

ALASKA | CANADA
Aleutian Islands

On the map
This map shows what was happening in America between 1590 and 1754. The Native Americans had been living on this land for thousands of years. Starting with the Jamestown settlement in Virginia in 1607, Europeans built colonies along the East Coast of North America. French explorers travelled America's waterways searching for a route to the Pacific Ocean and building settlements along the way.
By 1754, England and France claimed much of the continent. Spain, too, had claimed Florida and in the West. The arrows show what was traded by the colonies.

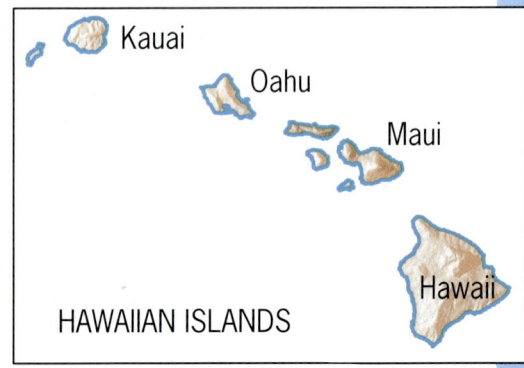

Kauai
Oahu
Maui
Hawaii
HAWAIIAN ISLANDS

42

ROCKY MOUNTAINS
PACIFIC OCEAN
Columbia
Snake
Missouri
Colorado
Colorado
Rio Grande
Santa Fe
El Paso

FISH → Trade Route
~ River
■ Spanish frontier lands in 1750
■ Spanish colonized by 1750
■ French frontier lands in 1750
■ French colonized by 1750
■ English frontier lands in 1750
■ English colonized by 1750
■ New Netherlands 1616

0   250   500 miles
0   400   800 kilometres

FURS • FISH (COD)
Hudson Bay
NEWFOUNDLAND
Champlain 1608
C A N A D A
St. Lawrence
Quebec
Lake Superior
Lake Champlain
MASSACHUSETTS
NEW HAMPSHIRE
LUMBER • COD • FURS
MANUFACTURED GOODS
Missouri
Marquette & Joliet 1673
Lake Huron
Lake Michigan
Lake Ontario
NEW YORK
Hudson
Salem
Boston
Plymouth
TOBACCO • RICE • INDIGO
Mississippi
Delaware
RHODE ISLAND
CONNECTICUT
Lake Erie
New York City
PENNSYLVANIA
Philadelphia
NEW JERSEY
DELAWARE
ATLANTIC OCEAN
MARYLAND
Missouri
VIRGINIA
Chesapeake Bay
Ohio
James
Jamestown
APPALACHIAN MOUNTAINS
Roanoke Island
NORTH CAROLINA
SOUTH CAROLINA
La Salle 1682
GEORGIA
Mississippi
Mission San Jose
New Orleans
SUGAR • MOLASSES
RUM • IRON
SLAVES
Rio Grande
GULF OF MEXICO
C U B A
HISPANIOLA
MEXICO
JAMAICA
CARIBBEAN SEA
SLAVES

Famous People of the Time

William Bradford, 1590–1657, was the second governor of the Plymouth Colony. He was re-elected 30 times.

John Carver, 1576–1621, was the first governor of the Plymouth Colony.

Samuel de Champlain, 1567–1635, was a French explorer who claimed parts of Canada and northern America for France.

Thomas West De la Warr, 1577–1618, was the first governor of the Virginia Colony. In 1610, he helped it survive its shaky beginnings. The river and state of Delaware are named after him.

John Endecott, 1588–1665, was a Puritan leader who founded Salem, the first settlement in the Massachusetts Bay Colony in 1628.

Benjamin Franklin, 1706–1790, was a leading citizen of Philadelphia, an author and publisher, and a famous inventor.

Thomas Hooker, 1586–1647, was a Puritan minister who left Massachusetts and founded the Connecticut Colony in 1636.

Anne Hutchinson, 1591–1643, was banished from Massachusetts Bay Colony in 1637 because of her religious views. She helped to settle the village of Portsmouth in Rhode Island.

Louis Joliet, 1645–1700, was a French explorer who explored the Mississippi River with Jacques Marquette and claimed much of the area for France.

Robert La Salle, 1643–1687, was a French explorer. He travelled the Mississippi River to the Gulf of Mexico and claimed the land around it as Louisiana.

Jacques Marquette, 1637–1675, was a French missionary and explorer who explored the Mississippi River with Louis Joliet.

Metacomet, ?–1676, also called King Philip, was chief of the Wampanoag Native Americans. He led a massacre of English settlers.

Peter Minuit, 1580–1638, purchased Manhattan Island for the Dutch in 1626 and started the settlement of New Amsterdam (today New York City). In 1638, Sweden asked him to start the colony of New Sweden on the Delaware River.

Important Dates and Events

THE COLONIES IN NORTH AMERICA
1603 Samuel de Champlain explores the St Lawrence River in Canada
1607 the English arrive at Jamestown, Virginia
1609 the winter called the Starving Time in Jamestown
1610s the first group of Black Africans are brought to North America as slaves
1619 Black Africans arrive in Virginia as indentured servants
1620 the *Mayflower* arrives and begins the Plymouth Colony
1622 Jamestown massacre leaves hundreds of colonists and Native Americans dead
1624 the Dutch start settlements in New Netherlands
1628 Salem is founded, as the first town in the Massachusetts Bay Colony
1634 Maryland is founded
1636 Connecticut is founded
1641 Massachusetts legalizes certain forms of slavery
1644 Rhode Island is founded
1660 Virginia begins passing laws to organize slavery
1663 Carolina is founded
1664 The English take over New Netherlands. New Jersey becomes a separate colony from New York.
1673 Marquette and Joliet explore the St Lawrence River, Great Lakes, and Mississippi River
1675 King Philip's War is started by Wampanoag Native Americans
1679 New Hampshire is founded
1681 Pennsylvania is founded
1682 Robert La Salle reaches the Gulf of Mexico on the Mississippi River and claims Louisiana for France
1703 Delaware becomes a separate colony from Pennsylvania
1704 *The Boston News-Letter* becomes the first successful newspaper in the colonies
1720 San José Mission is built in San Antonio, Texas
1732 Georgia is founded. The first stagecoach line runs between Burlington and Amboy, New Jersey.
1754 Ben Franklin presents the Plan of Union. The plan is not accepted.

James Oglethorpe, 1696–1785, founded the colony of Georgia as a settlement for poor, jobless people from England.

William Penn, 1644–1718, was the founder of the Pennsylvania colony for a religious group called the Quakers.

Pocahontas, 1596–1617, was a Native American princess who helped keep peaceful relations between Virginia settlers and the Powhatan tribe.

Powhatan, ?–1618, was chief of the Powhatan tribe, near the Jamestown, Virginia, settlement. His Native American name was Wahunsonacock.

Red Jacket, 1750?–1830, was an Iroquois Native American leader who opposed the efforts of missionaries and other white people who wanted to change his tribe's culture and way of life.

John Rolfe, 1585–1622, was a Jamestown colonist who introduced tobacco to the colony and married Pocahontas.

John Smith, 1580–1631, was a leader in the Jamestown colony and friend of Pocahontas.

Squanto, 1585–1622, was a Patuxet Native American who helped the Pilgrims survive at the Plymouth Colony.

Peter Stuyvesant, 1610–1672, was a Dutch leader of New Netherlands.

Sebastián Vizcaíno, about 1560–1610, was a Spanish explorer who named several landmarks along California's coast. In 1602, he urged Spain to colonize California before the English claimed it.

Roger Williams, 1603–1683, was a Puritan minister who believed in religious freedom. He was born in London and went to America in 1631. He was banished from Massachusetts Bay Colony along with Anne Hutchinson. Williams built a settlement in Providence, Rhode Island.

John Winthrop, 1588–1649, was the first governor of the Massachusetts Bay Colony. He helped found the city of Boston.

? means that historians are not sure of the exact date.

POCAHONTAS
1596 Pocahontas is born
1607 meets John Smith
1609 John Smith returns to England
1613 Pocahontas is kidnapped and is baptized with the name Rebecca
1614 Pocahontas marries John Rolfe
1615 Pocahontas gives birth to a son, Thomas
1616 Pocahontas goes to London with her husband and son
1617 Pocahontas dies on her way back to Virginia. She is buried at Gravesend in England.

CENTRAL & SOUTH AMERICA
1608 Paraguay is founded
1609 first English settlement on Bermuda
1625 French establish a port in Guiana
1629 English settle the Bahamas
1636 Dutch Guiana is founded
1648 French establish colonies in the West Indies
1655 England gets Jamaica from Spain
1742 Peruvian Native Americans revolt against Spanish rule

THE REST OF THE WORLD
1593–1613 In England, William Shakespeare writing his plays.
1607 first opera, by Italian composer Monteverdi
1618 start of 30 Years' War in Germany
1600–1700 England, France, Russia, and the Netherlands set up colonies in the East Indies
1600–1683 decline of the Ottoman Empire in Asia
1600–1700 Ashanti, Oyo, and Kongo kingdoms in Africa
1627–1707 Mogul Empire in India
1642–1648 English Civil War
1644 in China, Ming dynasty ends and Manchu dynasty starts
1660–1715 France becomes the dominant power in Europe, led by Louis XIV, the 'Sun King'
1680s Rise of the Austrian and Prussian empires in Europe
1689-1725 Rule of Peter the Great in Russia
1741 Russia explores Alaska

GLOSSARY

apprentice young person who agrees to work with – and often lives with – a skilled adult for some years to learn a trade

baptize pour water on someone's head or immerse someone in water in a ceremony to become a Christian

claim announce that something belongs to you or your country

colonist someone who lives in a newly settled place

colony place where settlers live far from the country that governs them

Dutch people from the European country known as Holland or the Netherlands

elected chosen by being voted for

engraving artwork made by cutting into metal, wood or glass surface

enslave make someone become a slave

entreaty attempt to change someone's mind

Great Plains land between the Mississippi River and the Rocky Mountains – the eastern part is often called the Prairies

harbour body of water where ships can come for shelter and to load and unload cargo

immigrant someone who moves from another country

longhouse large house in which several Native American families live

mission settlement of religious teachers, which includes a farm, church and other buildings

missionary someone sent by a church to teach religion in a foreign place

pen name made-up name used by an author

petticoat type of skirt worn by women underneath a dress

plantation large farm

rawhide skin of animals before it is soaked in a solution and made into leather

representative someone who acts and speaks for many people to help make laws

rituals ceremonies or customs which are often repeated in the same way

rum alcoholic drink made from sugar cane

self-government government which allows people the right to choose their leaders and make their laws

servant person who works for someone else for a certain period of time, often living in their employer's house or on their farm

settlement small village

settler person who makes a home in a new place

shingle small, thin pieces of building material which are laid in overlapping rows to cover a roof

slave person who is owned by another person and is usually made to work for that person

smoke cook meat over a smoky fire in a smokehouse to keep it from spoiling

stagecoach carriage pulled by horses, for travelling long distances which stopped off at 'staging posts' for the horses and passengers to rest

tax money paid to a government and used to run a town, state or country

trading post place where people trade goods with the people who live in the area

tribe group of people who share a territory, language, customs and laws

vaccine something injected into the body or swallowed which protects a person from getting a disease

weatherboard wood board used for siding on a house, narrower at one edge than the other

West Indies group of islands in the Atlantic Ocean stretching between Florida and South America

MORE BOOKS TO READ

Living Through History: The Making of the United Kingdom. N. Kelly, R. Rees, J. Shuter. Heinemann.

Native American Stories. Robert Hull. Wayland.

The Peoples of North America. Christine Hatt. Evans.

The Voyages of Discovery. Macdonald Young Books.

PLACES TO VISIT

The National Maritime Museum
   Greenwich
   London

The British Museum
   Ethnography Department (formerly the separate
   Museum of Mankind)
   Great Russell Street
   London

Liverpool Maritime Museum
   Albert Dock
   Liverpool

Bristol Maritime Heritage Centre
   Gas Ferry Road
   Bristol

INDEX

African culture 39
Africans 16, 38, 44
Algonquin 7
Atlantic Ocean 27, 38, 46

beads 8–9, 12, 24
beans 12, 28, 36
Boston 5, 20, 32–33, 45
Bradford, William 18–19, 44
buffalo 5, 28–29

California 30–31, 45
Canada 26–27, 44
Carver, John 19, 44
Champlain, Samuel de 27, 44
children 6–7, 18, 20, 23, 36, 38, 41
Christianity 14, 26, 30, 46
church 10, 12, 15, 18, 23, 30–31, 35, 46
city life 40–41
clocks and clockmakers 35
clothing 6–7, 14, 20, 32, 40–41
coins 32–33
colonies 5, 8–9, 12, 17, 19, 20–21, 24–26, 28, 36, 38, 40–42, 45–46
colonists 8, 12, 15–17, 22–23, 36, 38, 45–46
Connecticut 25, 44
cooking 18, 20–21, 23, 29, 39
corn and maize 6–10, 12, 14, 19, 25, 28, 36
cows 22, 31, 36
crop planting 7–8, 20, 36
customs 14, 30, 46

dance and ceremony 6–7, 31

De la Warr, Thomas 44
Delaware 25, 44
disease 16, 35, 38
doctors 12, 35
Dutch, the 24–25, 36, 44, 46

elections 17
Endecott, John 44
England 5–6, 8–9, 14–18, 20, 22, 32, 40, 42, 45
English, the 7–8, 10–11, 14, 23–25, 44–45
Equiano, Olaudah 38
Europe 25, 38, 46
explorers 5, 24, 26–27, 30, 42, 45

families 5, 10, 17, 20, 22–23, 36, 38
farming 8, 28, 30, 36–37
farms 16, 27, 30, 36, 46
fashion 24, 40–41
fighting 6, 11–12 16, 23, 28
fishing 6, 19, 33
Florida 30, 42, 46
food 7–9, 12, 18, 30, 36–37
forests 6, 10–11, 16
France 5, 26–27, 32, 42, 44
Franklin, Benjamin 34–35, 40–41, 44
freedom 16, 18–19, 28, 30, 38, 40
French, the 26–27, 30
fur trade 24, 27, 38

gardens 17, 22, 40
Georgia 25, 44–45
Germans, the 36
gold 6, 8, 16
Great Lakes 27, 44
Great Plains 28–29, 46
Gulf of Mexico 26–27, 44
guns 8, 10–11, 25

Index

heat and light 20
heating 34
Hooker, Thomas 44
horses 15, 22, 28–29, 31–32, 36
Hudson, Henry 24
hunting 5–6, 8, 28–29
Hutchinson, Anne 44

inventions 34
Ireland 36
Iroquois 30, 45

James River 5, 8
Jamestown 7, 12, 15–16, 42, 44–45
Joliet, Louis 27, 44

La Salle, Robert 26–27, 44
land 10, 17, 22–23, 26, 28, 36, 42
language 9, 24, 28
laws 17, 19, 23, 38, 44
lending libraries 34, 41
London 6, 8, 12, 14–15, 45
Louisiana 27, 44

mail and post 34, 41
Manhattan Island 24, 44
Marquette, Jacques 27, 44
Maryland 25, 44
Massachusetts 18–21, 25, 33, 38, 44
Massachusetts Bay Colony 20, 22–23, 44–45
Mayflower, 18–19, 44
meat 8, 29, 36–37
medicine 35
merchants 36–37, 38
Metacomet 23
Mexico 28, 44
Minuit, Peter 44
missionaries 30, 45–46
Mississippi River 26–28, 44, 46
Montreal 26–27

Native Americans 4–6, 8–11, 14, 16–17, 19, 23–24, 26–31, 42, 44–45
Netherlands 5, 24, 46
New Jersey 24–25, 35, 40, 44
New Netherlands 24–25, 44–45
New York 24, 35, 41, 44
newspapers 33–34, 44

Oglethorpe, James 45
Ontario, Lake 26

Pacific Ocean 27, 42
Penn, William 40, 45
Pennsylvania 25, 35–36, 41, 44–45
Philadelphia 5, 34–35, 40–41, 44
Pilgrims 18–19, 45
plantations 5, 16–18, 38–39, 46
Plymouth Colony 18–20, 23, 44–45
Pocahontas 4–6, 9–12, 14–16, 45
police 41
Powhatan tribe 5–10, 15, 45
Powhatan, Chief 6–7, 10–12, 14–15, 45
Puritans 18, 20, 23, 44, 45

Quakers 40, 45
Quebec 27

reading and writing 23, 30, 39
Red Jacket 30, 45
religion 18–20, 24–25, 30–31, 40, 44–46
Rhode Island 25, 44–45
rivers 6–7, 24, 26–27
Rolfe, John 14–15, 45

Salem 20, 44

schools 23, 31, 40
servants 20, 32, 37, 41, 46
settlements 15–16, 27, 42, 44–46
settlers 4–5, 7, 9–10, 12, 14, 20, 28, 44–46
silver 32–33, 37
slavery 16, 38–39, 41, 44–45
smallpox 14–15, 35
Smith, John 7, 9–12, 15, 19
South Carolina 25, 38–39
Spain 5, 32, 42, 45
Spanish, the 28, 30
Squanto 45
St Lawrence River 27, 44–45
stagecoach 35, 44, 46
'Starving Time' 12, 44
stores 23, 32–33, 40–41
Stuyvesant, Peter 25, 45
sugar 33, 36
swords 10–12

taxes 40, 46
tea 33, 36
teachers 23, 46
tepees 28–29
Thanksgiving 19
timber 21, 33
tobacco 14–17, 38, 45
towns 5, 22–24
trade 9–10, 12, 17, 27, 38
trading posts 24, 27, 46
tradition 10, 30
turkeys 6, 12, 36

United States of America 4, 20, 25
university 41

vaccine 35, 46
vegetables 6, 28, 31, 36

Virginia 5–6, 8, 10, 15–17, 25, 38, 41, 44–45
Vizcaíno, Sebastián 45

Wampanoag 19, 23, 44
war 23, 25
water 9, 10, 12
West Indies 38, 45–46
Williams, Roger 45
Winthrop, John 22, 45
women 6–7, 14, 16, 32, 36, 38, 40–41